MW01131796

Million Name Munson
Copyright © 2023 by Jaime Hoffman

All rights reserved. No part of this publication may be reproduced, distributed, or transmitted in any form or by any means, including photocopying, recording, or other electronic or mechanical methods, without the prior written permission of the author, except in the case of brief quotations embodied in critical reviews and certain other non-commercial uses permitted by copyright law.

Tellwell Talent
www.tellwell.ca

ISBN
978-1-77941-259-1 (Hardcover)
978-1-73805-250-9 (Paperback)
978-1-77941-260-7 (eBook)

Come, join in an adventure with a special little hound, who has acquired many names that can be goofy, nutty, or even make a funny sound!

Silly or fitting? You get to decide, which name suits her best as you read and enjoy the ride!

MILLION Name MUNSON

STORY and ILLUSTRATIONS
JAIME HOFFMAN

Hi! My name is Edna. Is that not strange, since the name of the book says Munson? For an explanation, turn the page...

You see, my Mom likes words, rhyming, and fun! She molds my name like cookie dough, and it turns out, not like it had begun.

I am named after a little lady with the last name **Mode.** My mom started changing it like her own secret code...

Soon, **Mode** became **Modeson,** which wasn't so new. But then she flipped it to **Munson,** which stuck like glue!

When I was very little I loved to sniff – to bury
my face in the grass and take a big whiff!

Mom noticed right away and scratched
her head like a wig. Then came
another name, **The Truffle Pig!**

Now, I'm a little schnauzer and not sure
if you're aware... I've got a bark so high
pitched you'll clench your teeth in despair.

Credit for this name goes to my Dad,
who dubbed me **Screaming Mendez**,
the loudest pooch in the land!

I'm tiny but stocky, not at all frail – a sturdy little box with a hint of a tail! Four names are a lot for a small dog like me.

Just jokes, there are more... wait and see!

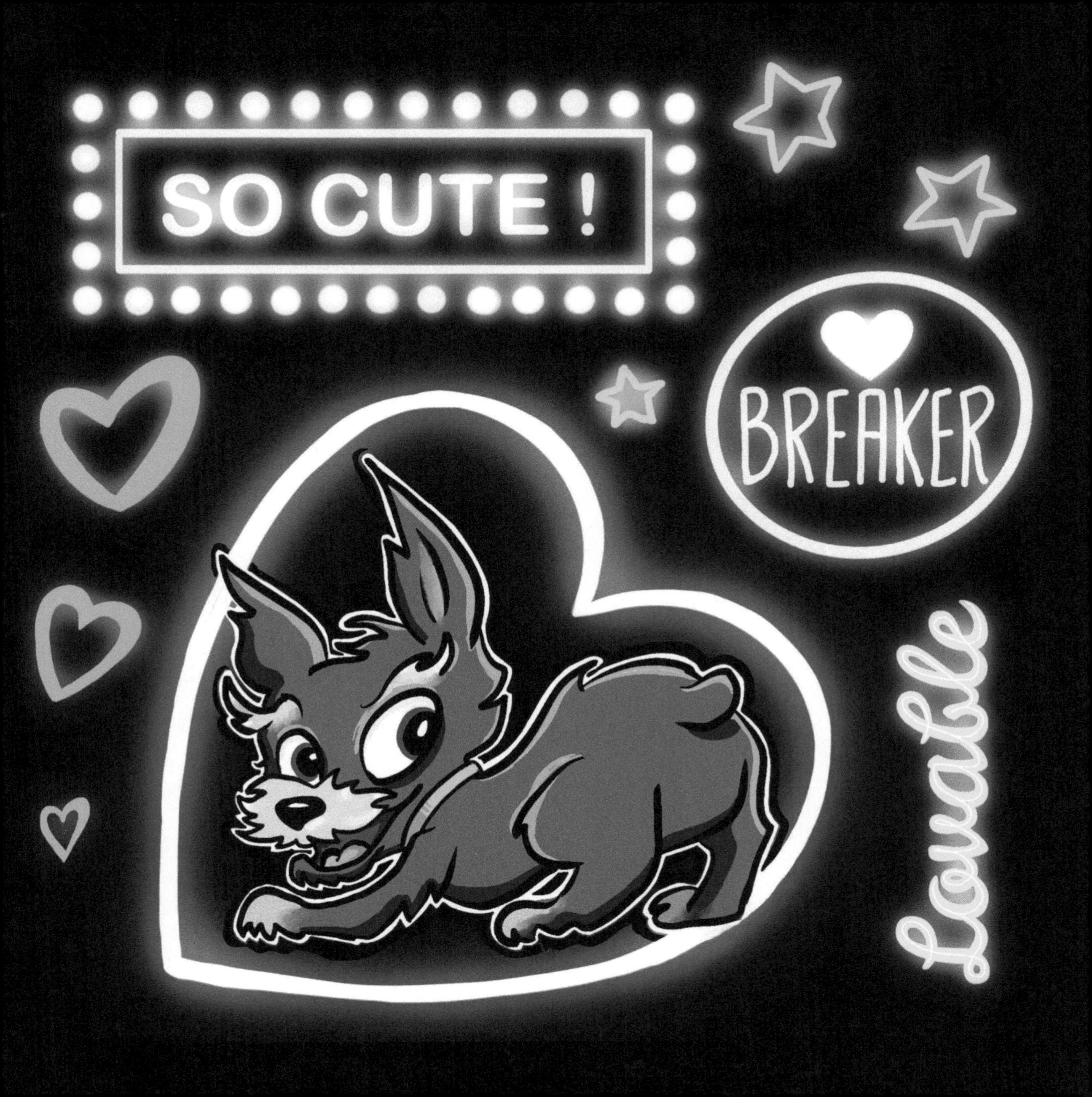
SO CUTE !
BREAKER
Lovable

Some of my names have no reason
at all – just fun to say and roll
off your tongue like a ball.

One summer Mom called me a name that
would stick in your mind. I am the glorious
Min-Win and I am one of a kind!

Sometimes things get unusual, creative at the least – the names they can come up with for just a regular beast...

Could this name make me feel like I know a martial art? A name like **Mat-Su-Ah Bamboo-Ah** is an excellent start!

The next name is cute and makes me feel
sweet, like I'm a tiny dog fairy you'd like to meet.

What does it mean? I really don't know. But
when Mom calls me **Pimm,** it makes me glow.

The latest name is descriptive but
short and sweet. It gives you a warning
if it is in your bed, I sleep...

Be prepared to be warm, maybe even
roasting! Because they call me **Paste**
as I lay against you hot and toasty.

So, that is just a handful of my million names!
Each one is special and never the same...

So, if you wonder if I know them
or do I comprehend? Just get my
Mom to yell **MUNSON!** and I'll
come running around the bend!

This book is dedicated to Edna and
the fisherman behind her.

Printed in the USA
CPSIA information can be obtained
at www.ICGtesting.com
LVHW060758140124
768912LV00043B/1675